WHAT THE NIGHT IS FOR

for Kathy

Michael Weller

WHAT THE NIGHT IS FOR

OBERON BOOKS
LONDON

First published in 2002 by Oberon Books Ltd.
(incorporating Absolute Classics)
521 Caledonian Road, London N7 9RH
Tel: 020 7607 3637 / Fax: 020 7607 3629

e-mail: oberon.books@btinternet.com
www.oberonbooks.com

A catalogue record for this book is available from the British
Library.

ISBN: 1 84002 355 4

Cover photograph: Lorenzo Agius

Image design: M + H Communications Ltd

Printed in Great Britain by Antony Rowe Ltd, Chippenham.

Characters

MELINDA METZ
a teacher of Special Education

ADAM PENZIUS
an architect

Both Adam and Lindy are in their mid- to late-forties.

What the Night is For was first produced by Act Productions, Sonia Friedman Productions and LHP at the Comedy Theatre, London on 7 November 2002 with the following cast and creative team:

MELINDA METZ, Gillian Anderson

ADAM PENZIUS, Roger Allam

Director, John Caird

Designer, Tim Hatley

Lighting Designer, Paul Pyant

Company Manager, Wyn Howard-Thomas

A note on punctuation

A slash / indicates a half expressed thought broken into or subverted by a following thought. Ordinarily a comma would do the trick, but a comma strikes me as indicating a purposeful aside or modification of a continuous and coherent thought. A slash indicates something more haphazard and inadvertant, plus it suggests that the phrase before it might stop altogether.

MW

ACT ONE

Scene 1

A hotel room somewhere.

Darkness. Pop – a champagne cork. Laughter.

Lights up on a room decorated in a bland traditional style. We could be in any of the better chain hotels in a mid-sized Midwestern city.

LINDY and ADAM sit at a table eating a meal off a trolley with silver domes. A hanging fixture over the table closes them in a tight embrace of light. Another lamp on one side of the double bed is on low beside a digital alarm/radio.

LINDY is full-figured with soft features. Her voice is quietly cadenced but she has sudden bursts of infectious mirth. She wears a tastefully stylish suit. ADAM has thinning hair and an easy but at times brisk efficient manner; a man used to giving orders. He's in tie and shirtsleeves, jacket flung on bed.

Both are in their mid-/late-forties. The mood is upbeat but a little shrill, each trying too hard to appear relaxed.

LINDY: (*Guessing.*) Millman? Hillman? Spillman, Spellman?

ADAM: No.

LINDY: Don't tell me, don't – Gellman. It was Gellman, right?

ADAM: (*Having fun.*) Nope.

LINDY: He was an ear-nose-and-throat man –

ADAM: Yes –

LINDY: With a hideous wife.

7

ADAM: Yes –

LINDY: Isn't she the one who got drunk that time and said we should skip the book discussion and try group sex for a change?

ADAM: That's the one.

LINDY: His name was Gellman, I'm sure it was. That week was 'Bonfire of the Vanities'.

ADAM: Right book, wrong doctor. Gasarch. Dr Gasarch.

LINDY: You know, I think you're right. He tried to grope me in the hallway my first night in the Book Circle. Well, doctors tend to be pretty biological on the whole. Don't you find?

ADAM: (*Absurdly.*) On the whole, absolutely.

LINDY: (*Giggles.*) Do you still see any of that bunch –

ADAM: The Get-A-Life Culture Club?

LINDY: Were they that pathetic?

ADAM: Present company excepted.

LINDY: Thank you.

ADAM: Actually, I did run into, was that obstetrics guy before your time – Dr Nicklaus? – vacation in Bora Bora at one of those, what are they, along the beach, open side thatched roof bar type things. He introduced me to a little dark haired cutie pie young enough to be someone he just delivered. His wife, he called her. The only good joke he ever told.

LINDY raises her champagne glass.

LINDY: A toast; to the Book Circle.

ADAM: And all that came of it! (*They click glasses.*) Tattinger. You remembered.

LINDY: I did? Oh… (*Then.*) Remembered what?

ADAM: My favourite champagne.

LINDY: It's the little touches that do a perfect hostess make.

ADAM: You *didn't* remember?

LINDY: I'm sure I did. Sub-thing-a-mally. You've barely touched your fish.

ADAM: Ditto your meat.

They take bites with awkward movements.

LINDY: How is it?

ADAM: My fish is fine. How's your meat?

LINDY: Good, actually. Quite succulent and, um – tender – (*Hearing innuendo.*) Oh dear, oh dear, Adam Penzius!

ADAM: Your nose still turns red when you blush.

LINDY: (*Busying herself with food.*) So tell me all about yourself. How's your – you know, everything, life. You talk while *I* eat, then we'll switch round and I'll provide the ambient sound while you tackle your fish. How's that for a plan?

ADAM: You haven't changed, Lindy.

LINDY: It's a little warm though, isn't it? The hotel said they're testing a new air conditioning system… I'll open a window, why don't I do that, I'll just – Aren't you warm? Aren't I babbling?

ADAM: I guess we're nervous.

LINDY: A little.

ADAM: Understandably.

LINDY: I'll just / It *is* warm…

She goes to the window.

ADAM rises.

A boy was it? How old?

ADAM almost calls her on this, then takes his jacket from the bed and removes some photos.

She turns.

They're awkwardly close in the middle of the room.

ADAM: (*Showing her a photo.*) Roo.

LINDY: Roo? For Rudolf?

ADAM: For Roo. As in 'Kanga and – .' From Winnie the Pooh. He curls up in my lap at breakfast, snuggles under my bathrobe like a baby kangaroo.

LINDY: He's ten?

ADAM: Clinging to his youth. Greg's his real name; Gregory.

So there they are, inches apart.

LINDY feels a wave of something and moves back to the table.

What were yours again?

LINDY: Same as before; Doug and Bill.

ADAM: (*Manly voice.*) That's right; 'The Guys'.

He returns to the table and sits.

LINDY: They are that, regular little jocks. Not so little now. Not completely jock, either, though Hugh does his best to push them that way. Football, baseball, basketball, anything with balls. *La Maison Testosterone,* that's what I call home. Is that your wife in the doorway?

He looks puzzled and half turns towards the door behind him.

LINDY grins, eyeing the photo beside ADAM's plate.

In the picture.

ADAM looks at the photo.

ADAM: (*Surprised.*) Oh, yes. Yes, that's – yes.

LINDY: What's *she* like?

He studies the picture, sets it aside.

ADAM: Oh, she's / she went back to work.

LINDY: That's what she's *like?*

ADAM: No, I mean – Career happens to be her focus right now, is all I – meant / – when you asked –

He lifts the photo again, glances at it, puts it down, then brings it to his coat on the bed to put it away, all with abstracted movements, mind and body running separately.

She earned a break after all those years full-time-momming it. You lose momentum in the job market, dancers especially, well, women in general – which is why she ended up starting her own business. It's an incredible amount of work, but it's finally paying off. Direct Marketing, that's her – field / Selling lists of buyers to various sellers. Interested in finding buyers. To sell to. So, anyway. Yeah, she travels a lot.

LINDY sets down her napkin. He is sitting.

LINDY: And you're home with Greg?

ADAM: I really love being with him. Almost more than anything.

LINDY: I never thought you'd marry – 'Jan', was it?

11

ADAM: Why not?

LINDY: Living together all that time, six years?

ADAM: Nine-ish. Actually.

LINDY: Could be seen as a sign of, oh, ambivalence?

ADAM: More a sign of the times; too busy with other things.

LINDY: Well, Adam. Quite the snazzy life you lead. Travelling architect. With travelling wife. Each with their own business, his and hers, just like towels. Plus a cute little boy. (*Beat.*) A nanny?

ADAM: Of course. (*Playing her game.*) And a brownstone, a summer place in Pennsylvania, all the trimmings.

LINDY: Sounds…nice.

ADAM: It is, actually. It's really nice.

LINDY: Well…good.

ADAM: And you?

LINDY: (*Shrugs.*) Ooo-blah-dee, life goes on. More bubbly?

Both start to rise.

ADAM: *I'll* pour.

LINDY: My hotel room, you're the guest. (*She pours for them both.*) Actually, I *like* playing hostess. Trained from girlhood, you know. Cranbook Juniors. All us marriageable gals were sent there to master etiquette and comportment, not to mention HomeEc and floral arrangement. The essentials.

ADAM: I never pegged you as the hostess type. The way you were in New York I'd have thought –

LINDY: New York was a parenthesis. Before and after is the real me.

ADAM: What's tonight; parenthesis, or real?

LINDY: Tonight – (*She stops, blushing.*) Well. You called. Cheers.

They clink glasses across the table.

ADAM: So, are there Book Circles out here?

LINDY: In the Midwest, you mean? You'd be surprised by the amenities 'out here'. We have electricity, Supermarkets, copycat crime…

ADAM: I didn't mean it that way. (*Sees her smile.*) Like some condescending New York asshole.

LINDY: Should I order a second bottle?

ADAM: You're so damn lovely. (*Then.*) Sorry.

He looks down, abashed.

LINDY: You've held up pretty well yourself.

The sudden attraction overwhelms them both.

(*Quick, sing-song.*) Is that fold-out sofa still in the conference room?

ADAM: (*Welcoming the change of pace.*) The client couch? The Famous Aztec Hippie Folding Futon?

LINDY: God, wasn't it hideous. Did your wife chose it?

ADAM: My wife?

LINDY: No one with taste could've chosen something like that so I figured it must be a concession to family. Or a charitable gesture to the sight impaired.

ADAM: My partner's wife, in fact. During her 'liberated' phase. She threatened to leave him, so he validated her

13

'aesthetic side' by putting her on salary as a interior design consultant. The sofa's long gone.

LINDY: And the wife?

ADAM: Also gone; Key West, lives with a janitor on a houseboat! Life!

ADAM shakes his head in wonderment, backing into a world of feelings bigger than he's ready for.

LINDY: Ooblah-dee. I was surprised to hear from you.

Okay, time to deal with it.

ADAM: It never crossed your mind I might one day…?

LINDY: Why now? What made you – (*She stops.*)

ADAM: A job was taking me near your neck of the woods / seemed like a chance to catch up.

LINDY: After eleven years?

ADAM: (*With a slight edge.*) Well, it wasn't *me* who upped and left New York without saying any– (*Stops.*) I never knew for sure if you'd want to hear from me.

LINDY composes herself to answer.

LINDY: I apologise. It *was* abrupt, yes. Things sort of *erupted* one day; Hugh's dad, him racing back here for the funeral, to run the company. And I had the whole family to pack, the kids. Not to mention ready myself to meet the Metz clan for the first time. It was…chaos.

ADAM: It would have helped to know that.

LINDY: Of course. I acted thoughtlessly. The Cranbrook Juniors would not approve of how I handled our / actually, I don't think / *is* there an established etiquette for ending a fling?

ADAM: (*Irritated.*) Fling?

LINDY: (*Conceding.*) Okay, 'affair'?

ADAM: Is that what it was?

LINDY: When a married woman with two young children
and a married man – well, *almost*-married, cohabiting for
nine-ish years, *Jan* is it?

ADAM: (*Cutting through.*) You know perfectly well.

LINDY: (*Quickly.*) When you meet in secret after Book
Circle and end up naked on a futon in his office / loft for
hours and hours, isn't that exactly the meaning of, yes,
'affair'. (*Then.*) Torrid affair? Is that better?

ADAM: Your nose is red.

LINDY: (*Smiling.*) You're getting a meal out of my guilt.
And the food here isn't cheap, believe me.

ADAM: And we *are* in your room.

LINDY: I should explain that –

ADAM: No need…

LINDY: I'm expecting a call.

ADAM: From your husband?

LINDY: (*Hesitating.*) No, actually…from Keeshon.

ADAM: Should I know that name?

LINDY: He's just a kid – (*Then.*) No, actually he's an
amazing kid. He was drawing on the sidewalk one day,
you know, chalk; this huge picture of a baby with a red
blob where the head should be. I asked him why the
head was that colour. 'It's his mouff wide open crying
blood cause he alone.' So I gave him a few dollars to
draw me some pictures…food money, really. He's

homeless. Eleven years old. Dad shot him in the chest for crying too loud when he was five. Anyway, it all got out of hand…he called me one night from jail and I had to arrange for his release. Since then I've become his safety net. And I don't know how to get out of it, I can't just walk away / well, I could – (*She stops.*)

ADAM: (*Lightly.*) And so here we are, in your room.

LINDY: If you saw his work you'd understand… He's a natural artist, goes right to the heart of it.

ADAM: Lindy, you don't have to explain yourself.

LINDY: Anyway, nights are hard for him, so he calls me if he needs to talk. And I'm out of town for the weekend, so… I gave him my number at the hotel.

ADAM: Okay. *That's* why we're here.

LINDY: Yes, Adam, that's why we're here.

ADAM: (*Since she won't leave it alone.*) And the cell-phone in your purse? You couldn't have given him *that* number? In case you wanted to dine out with me? Instead of in?

LINDY is caught at her elaboration.

LINDY: If I said it was broken, would you check?

ADAM: I'd wonder why the elaborate excuse for wanting to be alone with me?

LINDY thinks a moment, then decides to level.

LINDY: All right. Damn you, Adam. My family…my husband's family, they're…*prominent.* Metz bicycles, you know; after Schwinn, what else *is* there? And Hugo's weighing a run for state senate – and so, if Mrs Metz was seen dining with a strange man several hundred miles from home, a man not part of the education conference here…and word got back, which it definitely would, this is a very very small state... I'd have to explain 'the interesting-looking man I had dinner with last Saturday', and I'd get another lecture about political enemies looking for any hint of impropriety, etc, etc... I don't lie very well, I'm afraid; this darn nose.

ADAM: Why lie about having dinner with an old friend?

LINDY: Let's change the subject.

ADAM: What'd you tell him back in New York?

LINDY: That I was with devoted readers discussing books.

ADAM: Till two in the morning?

LINDY: He trusted me.

She revealed too much by careless wording.

ADAM picks up on it immediately.

ADAM: Trus*ted*?!

LINDY: Don't go there, Adam. (*Brighter, and a little too much energy.*) Does your boy ever say that? 'Hey, Doug, got a new girl friend?' 'Don't go there, mom.' Oh, and 'snap'. Everything cool is 'snap' now. Has that caught on back east? Or is it already old.

ADAM: My boy's still in the 'Buttbrain' phase; Vomit Breath. Penis Head. Doo-doo Face.

LINDY: (*Perks up.*) Oh, God, I *adored* that age, it was so, so *noisy* and *physical* and honest, isn't that what always goes on between people just under the surface – my husband watches C-Span, all these stuff shirt politicos – 'I object to the suggestion of my esteemed colleague from Texas', meaning 'Liar, Liar, Pants-on-Fire', or 'I'm morally opposed to the notion that –' when what they really *mean* is 'Up yours, Butt-Brain!'

LINDY realises he has become too animated for a moment, and backpedals.

(*Beat.*) One often feels.

She grows quiet, sips champagne, then bursts out laughing.

ADAM: *This* is how I remember you. Irreverent and breathless and blurting out anything that came to your mind. You seem so subdued tonight. Are you being *careful* with me? Or is this the before-and-after-New York Lindy?

LINDY: (*Beat.*) Eat your fish.

ADAM: No, let's *not* change the subject.

After a silence, the radio-alarm clicks on, filling the room with deafening music.

LINDY: Damn it, for two days that thing's been...excuse me.

She tries to turn it off, jiggling buttons, poking them, standing mystified.

How do I stop it?!

She pokes more buttons.

ADAM stands beside her and leans towards the gizmo.

ADAM: This one on the end works the alarm.

He lowers the sound. It's in fact a slow moody-blues. They straighten inches apart. The intimacy is overt and inescapable.

Did we ever dance?

LINDY: We skipped the preliminaries. If memory serves.

They stand like this for a moment.

ADAM: Never too late.

LINDY turns off the radio.

LINDY: I think I need a clearer idea of what's going on here before – more goes on.

ADAM: (*Flirting.*) We're having dinner. In your room. Because your nose might give you away if you tried explaining me to your husband. Who doesn't trust you like he used to.

Both burst out laughing at what is so clearly near the surface.

LINDY: (*Covering her nose shyly.*) Is it *very* red?

ADAM: Extremely.

LINDY grows animated, nervous, rearranging things on the table absently.

LINDY: Why aren't you *different*, Adam! Why don't you have a pot belly and, and you know, be irritable and wear thick glasses or something. Like this couple at my high school reunion, the husband you could smell his cheap aftershave across the room; and his shoulders were white with dandruff, he was all swollen-looking with this swollen wifey-person in a peach-coral-ish gown, an inflated Mid-Life Ken and Barbie and / but there was something about him, I don't know, he reminded me of *you.*

ADAM: Thank you so much.

LINDY: Maybe Adam looks like that, I thought. Swelling up, puffy and old. Which would make our whole episode, you know…easier to let go –

She is still fussing, not looking at him.

And then you called and your voice sounded the same, and – well, that can happen, voices stay young while the rest sags and droops…

Now she's still. She doesn't look at him.

I never expected… When you walked in – !

ADAM: Me, neither. I thought you'd be –

LINDY: No, I mean, Adam, you haven't changed is the thing. At all.

ADAM: And you're perfect.

LINDY: (*Shy.*) Yeah, right…

ADAM: When the door opened I thought: 'This is what she was growing towards. Now she's perfect.'

They stare at each other lost in possibilities.

LINDY turns away.

LINDY: How do things get so intense around you so very fast? You'd think after all this time…

She fans herself, comically relieving heat.

I mean – *whew*! (*Brighter.*) So, how long are you in town for? Did you say?

ADAM: I leave tomorrow night.

LINDY: Business.

ADAM: A client. Potential. If he approves my bid after the final presentation tomorrow. Which he will.

LINDY: He said quivering with self-doubt.

ADAM: I'm much in demand.

LINDY: So you just – decided to look me up?

ADAM avoids answering directly.

ADAM: More or less. This job's not my usual kind of bid, 'Environmentally Responsible Office Blocks of Visual

Distinction', meaning not too high and lots of trees. But it's big money, the work is A-B-C stuff, my assistants can handle most of it, so I figured I could buy a little freedom to polish a few projects for international competition.

LINDY: Good luck.

ADAM: Thank you.

The veil of small talk is wearing thin, but LINDY isn't ready for the next step.

LINDY: Shall we toast your what-is-it, final sales pitch?

She pours more champagne.

ADAM: (*Slightly huffy.*) 'Presentation'. It's called a –

LINDY: 'Presentation', sorry.

ADAM: (*Carefully.*) If I nail it, I'll have to make trips out here pretty often.

LINDY: Poor Adam. Mind you, there *are* diversions to be had. Just a stone's throw down the pike there's the celebrated Candy Bar Museum of North America, featuring the largest gumdrop in the world. It weighs several hundred pounds, they say. There's even a gift shop with miniature Gummie Bear key chains available nowhere else in the known universe.

ADAM: I was thinking more along the lines / maybe we could say hello from time to time.

LINDY: 'Hello'?

ADAM: Have lunch together.

LINDY: I don't live here, Adam, I'm attending a conference. Home is two hundred miles away.

ADAM: A short hop.

LINDY: (*A teasing smile.*) Two hundred miles? For lunch?

ADAM: Why not, if you were free.

LINDY: Neither of us is free.

ADAM: You know what I mean.

LINDY: Yes, and so on.

They sip and think for a moment.

ADAM: How early do you leave tomorrow?

LINDY: Seven am. US Air.

ADAM: There's nothing later? My final meeting's not 'til three. We could have – brunch.

LINDY: We have tonight.

ADAM: I see.

LINDY: Your food's getting cold.

ADAM: I'm not hungry.

LINDY: (*Suddenly lighter.*) Before I forget!

She brings him a tiny gift box from a shopping bag.

ADAM: What's the occasion?

LINDY: Just a Goofy Gift.

He holds the box, smiling at the memory.

ADAM: Oh my God. I've kept them all, you know. The ceramic shopping bag, the miniature abacus, the sailboat mobile –

LINDY: Open it.

ADAM open the box and unwraps lavender tissue paper; a tiny wooden jointed cow.

ADAM: (*Bewildered.*) A small…wooden…cow?

LINDY: Local folk art. Push the button underneath.

ADAM holds it up and pushes. The cow collapses.

(*Comical cow voice.*) 'My knees are weak! (*He pushes again.*) Mooo!!!'

ADAM: They always had a secret meaning, your Goofy Gifts. That ceramic paper bag, wasn't that to –

LINDY: To hold our secrets.

ADAM: And the abacus was to keep track of how many times –

LINDY: – in one night.

ADAM: What was the sailboat mobile, something about – ?

LINDY: Into the sunset. Happy endings.

ADAM: Of course, how could I forget. So this would be?

He pushes the button idly under the cow.

LINDY: (*In playful response.*) 'My knees, my kneeeeees!!!'

ADAM: (*Thinking.*) I push a button underneath and… (*Onto something.*) Ah, her knees grow weak. Am I warm?

LINDY: (*Flirting outrageously now.*) *I* am.

ADAM: Why a cow?

LINDY: They were sold out of the wife-and-mother adulterer models.

ADAM: (*Still unsure.*) Is the Goofy Gift for old time's sake? Or is it more a present tense kind of deal?

LINDY: Yes.

ADAM: Yes, *which*?

LINDY: (*Smiles.*) 'Moooo.'

ADAM: I'm assuming it's all right if I kiss you?

LINDY: Or we could talk about a book first, if that would help you relax. (*Teasing.*) Read anything good lately?

ADAM: (*Standing up.*) I just want to be sure.

She stands smoothing her dress.

They approach shyly, teenagers with a first kiss.

As they start to embrace, the alarm-radio goes off at deafening volume.

Damn it.

LINDY: Didn't you turn it off?

ADAM: I thought so.

He finds a button that makes it quieter by degrees. Then he turns to her.

They approach each other about to dance when the telephone rings.

LINDY: Oh, shit; Keeshon. I forgot. The music.

ADAM switches off the alarm/radio.

ADAM: Do you want privacy? Should I go in the / somewhere? / bathroom?

She signals 'stay', and picks up the phone.

ADAM crosses the room giving her privacy.

LINDY: Hello?

She is surprised by the voice she hears.

Oh... Hugh, I – / No, I was in the middle of – I was just eating dinner. / I didn't feel like going out, it's been a long day. / Very interesting so far…some unscheduled speakers… They talked about their field of expertise, darling, it's technical –

She seems a little irritated.

Has Doug done his homework? / He has to finish the paper *tonight*, Hugh, a make-up game tomorrow is no excuse / Football isn't going to make him more sociable, he's a *private* person, he's *thoughtful*, and playing mediocre football doesn't make him feel better about himself –

She takes her near-empty champagne glass from the table. The subject has been changed.

It's on top of the – / Why does he need a laxative, are you feeding him junk food? / Look in the medicine cabinet, top shelf. / And what about the casserole I left in the freezer, didn't you have it for dinner? / Pizza!!?? / No wonder he's constipated!

She looks apologetic for dragging ADAM through this mundane domesticity.

ADAM's raised eyebrow make her grin.

Is Willy there? Okay, when they get home give them a hug for me…a *manly* football hug.

She drains her champagne. She could use a bit more to get through the next step.

ADAM notices.

Well, actually, Hugh, I was thinking – there's a few elective sessions tomorrow / not part of the main conference, but the subjects interest me and I'd like to attend. There's an extra flight Sundays at – (*Referring to nothing.*) Let's see, four thirty-five, I could –

ADAM notes her 'act', and her almost empty champagne glass. While she speaks, he brings over the bottle, tips it up and finds it almost empty. So he pours his own champagne into her glass, an intimate gesture – all the while she talks to her husband.

Yes, I realise you'd miss your golf, for once in eleven years, but these are people who's work I should know better / *Who are they?* Specialists, Hugh, you wouldn't know them – / Dr Anna Weiss and Jacobo Boyle. / Hugh… I won't beg permission to stay an extra day, *part* of a day, actually / well, it feels like begging –

This is more outburst than she intended.

Thank you. / Remember, thaw the casserole before the football game. / There's a note on top how to cook it. / Me, too. Good night.

She hangs up. ADAM and LINDY's game with the champagne has created an intimacy between them.

(*Hand over nose.*) It must be glowing in the dark.

ADAM: Anna Weiss and Jacobo – ?

LINDY: *Boyle.* They're real. I could never make up names like that. Yes, I could. (*Then.*) The seminars are real.

ADAM: I thought you planned to leave in the morning.

LINDY: I did.

ADAM: Why memorise tomorrow's events?

LINDY: (*Silly question.*) As my son would say; duh!

ADAM: Will Hugh check your story?

LINDY: He already has, I bet. I left a conference schedule under some paperwork on my desk. He found it, felt clever and relieved and right about now he'll be starting to feel a little guilty that he didn't trust me.

ADAM: Your deceitfulness is impressively thorough.

LINDY: Thank you, and yours? If your wife calls your
hotel and you're…elsewhere?

ADAM: Why would she call?

LINDY: To say hello? Ask where you left the oatmeal soap?
I don't know, married stuff? She could just get lonely
and feel like talking.

ADAM: She doesn't get lonely.

LINDY: *Everyone* gets lonely.

ADAM: Some people don't know that's what it is. They
don't call. They – work.

LINDY: What if there's an emergency at home?

ADAM: Are you getting cold feet?

LINDY: I'm being careful, Adam. New York was playing
with matches. Now it's a big bonfire we have to watch
out for, two families and all.

ADAM: (*Lifting jacket.*) Beeper. I'm a dial tone away. (*He
moves to her. She turns away.*) What's wrong?

LINDY: I don't know. Something feels…odd.

ADAM: Unfamiliar? Ten years.

LINDY: No, I mean…what do I mean? I could always feel
your moods. You seem…hesitant. (*Then.*) When you
applied for the job here, did you know I lived nearby?

ADAM: (*Seemingly perplexed.*) That's a strange question.

LINDY: Did you?

ADAM: Why?

LINDY: (*Working it out.*) If you knew how close I lived –
and, I mean, you talked like this client wasn't your usual

27

kind of bid, so I'm wondering if you're after it for purely professional reasons or if I have something to do with, yes, that's what I mean, I'm worried that you *need* something you're not saying, something from me. Do you?

ADAM: (*Too casually.*) My secretary screwed up the hotel reservation so I went on-line to get things straight and – there it was, Metz Bicycles, on the web site, a Pop-Up with moving wheels…

LINDY: Yes, I know the logo, thank you.

ADAM: I put two and two together. Metz, of Lindy fame. You never said much about your personal life, but I remembered something about 'Hugo's Bicycle Fortune'. I did a search. Bingo.

LINDY: You just stumbled across my name.

ADAM: Pure accident.

LINDY: No hidden agenda.

ADAM: Plain old curiosity; how's she doing, what's she like now?

LINDY: Your once-upon-a-time mistress?

ADAM: We did have fun. Weren't you a little curious all these years? Isn't that why you're here?

LINDY: Actually… I came to get laid.

ADAM: (*Pause.*) Well. That's (*What?*) – clearcut.

LINDY: Only that, Adam. Nothing more.

ADAM: Just like old times.

LINDY: (*Takes up phone, watching ADAM.*) This is room 410. Hold my calls for tonight. Thank you.

LINDY puts down phone. She smiles, offering lightly –

Moo?

The lights dim.

Scene 2

A while later. LINDY and ADAM sit apart, she in an armchair facing away from him, he on the bed watching her. Both are dishevelled, flushed, and disoriented.

LINDY: What a mistake!

ADAM: Which part…?

LINDY: Taking your call, meeting you, everything, everything!

He watches her. The room is quiet.

Don't look at me.

ADAM: You're breathtaking.

LINDY: I'm a mess.

ADAM: You're in disarray.

LINDY: No, Adam, I'm a mess. Sorry about this.

Silence.

ADAM: That was some curve ball: 'I came to get laid.'

LINDY: Oh, yes, yes, trying to slip back in the old groove, A Walk on the Wild Side with Lindy Metz.

ADAM: What just happened?

LINDY: You mean 'happened twice', in rapid succession, with my clothes still on!

ADAM: Really?

LINDY: And nothing for you, poor Adam.

ADAM: At least one of us had fun. Twice.

LINDY: And I thought down there was all sort of…dead.

ADAM: Just sleeping?

LINDY: Yes. Like Sleeping Beauty, one kiss in the right place… (*Brighter.*) Maybe that's what that story's about, *all* fairy tales in fact, maybe they're about sexual awakening, sort of toddler versions of sex to plant a seed for later, when we're ready for the real thing.

ADAM: Lindy, anything that pops into your head right now's going to seem erotic.

She shivers with pleasurable memory.

LINDY: I mean, Sleeping Beauty; it's so *blatantly* sexual – / Here comes Sir Knight on his milky white stallion, 'Oh, look who's lying there on her back, waiting to be kissed, I bet if I pressed my knightly mouth against her soft lips why that little philly would buck and tremble right to life.' I mean, please. There's a book about this, right? Must be. 'Sex and the Fairy Tale'. Someone's already thought of it.

She is genuinely intoxicated by this idea, eager to 'discuss further'.

ADAM: I'll ask at the next Book Circle.

LINDY: (*Caught out.*) Oh. Am I trying to…? – yes I am / change the subject. I *am* sorry about all this, Adam.

ADAM: Never apologise for what happens between us.

His focus is intense.

She stands abruptly and speaks with too much animation.

LINDY: How would you like some ice water?

ADAM: I can think of nothing I'd like less.

LINDY: We can't sit around here for the rest of the night leaking. (*Mock hearty.*) We have to get hold of ourselves!

ADAM: (*Amused.*) '*Get hold* of ourselves?'

LINDY: Ice water's actually a very good way to –

ADAM: Put a chill on things.

LINDY: In fact.

ADAM: Fine. Ice water.

LINDY goes into the bathroom.

ADAM wanders the room, adjusting his anatomy.

LINDY speaks from in the bathroom, accompanied by sounds of running water.

LINDY: (*Off.*) Everything okay out there?

ADAM: Everything's honkey dory.

LINDY: (*Off.*) No swelling?

ADAM: (*Baffled.*) Swelling?!

LINDY: (*Off.*) From – having to stop prematurely?

ADAM: Why would there be…? What are you *talking* about!?

LINDY: (*Off.*) That *thing* that happens when men have to stop before they, um… Hugh said it's like a clogged drain that backs up and you swell – down there. It's very painful he says: Pink Balls, something like that?

ADAM shakes his head in disbelief, not sure she's putting him on.

ADAM: Blueballs?

LINDY: (*Off, laughs.*) Blue, that's right! I had this picture when he told me – little blue berries exploding on a bush. You don't have that, do you?

ADAM: My blueberries are fine, thank you.

LINDY stands in the door holding two glasses of water. She has fixed herself up again. With hair down and suit jacket off, and the light from the bathroom framing her, she looks achingly sensual.

LINDY: That was a close call.

ADAM: (*Smitten.*) Lindy – !

LINDY: (*Cutting him short.*) Ice?

She goes to the wet bar. ADAM tries to recover his equilibrium.

ADAM: So, Hugh told you about blueballs?

LINDY: (*Shyly.*) Sounds crude, I know. But I prefer to know these things. If he's in the mood and I'm not it's easy enough to just – assist him.

ADAM: May I ask you a question?

LINDY: (*Playfully arch.*) I think we've reached a point in the evening where questions can be entertained, yes.

ADAM: I assume you went to college?

LINDY: (*Puzzled.*) SMU.

ADAM: And you read books, magazines, keep up with current events?

LINDY: Why?

She whacks the ice tray once on the counter.

ADAM: Have you ever actually *heard* of a man swelling with pain 'down there' because a woman refused to go all the way?

She plops ice in both glasses, still trying to be light.

LINDY: Now that you mention it…

ADAM: (*Half indignant.*) Blueballs! That's from the dark ages of drive-in movies and bee-hive hairdos, guys used it to guilt-trip their dates into bed. You mean your husband, in all seriousness, told you –

LINDY: (*Terse.*) Yes, as I said, I am in certain respects, a little naive…

ADAM: A little?

LINDY: I wasn't raised to question things like that, Adam. I was taught to cultivate a look of fascination when a man spoke, but not listen too carefully. You met me at the tippy end of a thirty year slumber, speaking of Sleeping Beauty.

ADAM: You're the most baffling woman I ever met.

She grows increasingly rankled.

LINDY: Okay you made your point; I'm naive, you're worldly. I'm sorry I couldn't go through with it, that's me in my provincial place, moving right along – !

ADAM: (*Startled by her outburst.*) Calm down.

LINDY: (*Sharply.*) Never tell me to calm down! Never say that to me, ever!

She stops, amazed by her outburst.

(*Calmer now.*) I'm really sorry. On the bed before / it frightened me.

ADAM: Why?

LINDY: For a moment I couldn't remember my life.

ADAM: Isn't that supposed to happen, for a moment?

LINDY: Not like – (*Trying to pin it down.*) I was *back then*, in your office; *literally*, us on the futon. I was *there*, Adam, do you understand what I'm saying – like a needle you put back on a record just where you left off, but *years* later. Nothing that happened since then seemed real. I couldn't remember where I *am*. My life. Except vaguely – I'm married, I have children, I live somewhere not-New York. Part of my brain just dropped away. I panicked. I'm okay now. It was a deja thing. Vu. Deja-Voodoo. The old magic.

She sees the water glasses on the counter.

Ice water! (*Brings glasses over.*) Cheers.

ADAM: I prefer champagne.

They clink glasses and drink. The mood is dangerous and raw – anything might happen.

LINDY: So, tell me, Adam. Apart from tonight how's life?

ADAM: Oh, everything's by and large. And yours?

LINDY: (*Ruefully.*) I'm trying to recall.

ADAM: One more question?

LINDY: Something neutral, I hope.

ADAM: This 'fling' of ours – isn't that what you called it…pretty casual word for something that makes you panic eleven years later…even fully clothed.

LINDY: Oh. You want to strut, is that it?

ADAM: Was it a fling? Or more than a fling?

LINDY: Look, I'm fully aware – actually *painfully* aware – of the difference between your experience and mine / of our episode in New York.

ADAM: What difference is *that*?

LINDY: Adam, enough. I didn't put out. Okay. You're angry. You've embarrassed me. We're even.

ADAM: Why embarrassed?

LINDY: I think that's pretty obvious. Married matron plans torrid night with ex-lover, the simplest encounter on earth this side of Peyton Place, dinner sex and *au revoir*? And she can't even pull it off.

ADAM: Yes, I got that, but what's the problem?

LINDY: Too many memories. You bring back that whole year. The craziness, the excitement. All those amazing people –

ADAM: Like yourself?

LINDY: In my dreams.

ADAM: Lindy, you were head and shoulder above half the east village Pseuds I ran with. You were a published poet, for God sake.

LINDY: Not published; xeroxed, stapled in the corner and sold in three downtown bookstores run by pasty-looking macrobiotics with too much nostril hair.

ADAM: The Village Voice called you Emily Dickinson on Angel dust.

LINDY: 'Ecstasy', darling. Don't misquote my best and only mention in the annals of forgotten verse.

ADAM: (*Half-teasing.*) See, you even talk like a poet.

LINDY: I'm showing off for an appreciative audience; the first in years. (*Beat.*) You don't have to flatter me, darling. I was a small town debutante who had the very good luck to land a Hugo Metz. I didn't *need* poetry to say what I had to say, and what I had to say was ordinary. All in all, I'm a pretty ordinary woman.

35

ADAM: Bullshit.

She is becoming agitated now.

LINDY: Tell me, how many ex-mistresses do you have 'round the country? Are nights like this one of the perks of success?

ADAM: (*Irked.*) Don't try and wriggle off the hook for skipping out on me like that. If it was a casual fling, fine, let's hop into bed and screw for *Auld Lange Syne*. But if it meant enough for the memory to freak you out after all these years – I'm sorry, that's no casual fling, Lindy.

LINDY: We had an affair. Of course it meant *something!*

ADAM: Beyond the normal?

LINDY: What's 'beyond?' Indeed, what's 'normal?'

ADAM: Lindy, look at me.

LINDY: (*With rising anger.*) Well, my God, all right – what do *you* think? The way I gave myself, I'm not *that* shameless. Maybe other women you've known, but not this girl, not by a very long shot. I thought you were being tactful back then not mentioning how over the top I acted when we were together –

ADAM: I had no idea.

LINDY: Oh, please! You purred like a cat afterwards. You knew what you did to me. Look at my nose, for God sake, ten years later I'm still blushing at what a brazen whatever I was, groupie.

ADAM: Groupie? You?!

LINDY: Well, weren't you – what was the phrase 'the hottest, hippest, happening-est architect in TriBeCaStan?' – isn't that how Mirabella put it? And he developed a warm spot for, imagine, a young mother from below the Mason-Dixon line.

ADAM: How can you be so incredibly off base? First of all, I never *had* another 'mistress'. Second, 'purring'? I was dumbstruck lying with you, wondering how I ever lucked into a woman like – you were the most ravishing, mysterious person I ever / and with a real grown up life, two toddlers, a husband on Wall Street. And God knows what arrangement with him...

LINDY: You know, if I couldn't see your face right now I'd swear you were putting me on.

ADAM: I thought you got bored with me one day and found a new lover. It took me a year to work up the courage to track down your number.

LINDY: You called?

ADAM: The line was disconnected.

LINDY: This is so bizarre.

ADAM: I waited to hear from you. For a very long time.

LINDY: This *is* Adam Penzius I'm talking to, right? You don't have an evil twin who used to shave his head and wear lapel-less jackets? And waited by the elevator after my first book circle to whisper in my ear 'Come with me right now.'

ADAM: I'd never done something like that before in my life. Or since.

LINDY: (*Studies him a moment, then.*) Adam, stop it, stop teasing, I'm embarrassed...

ADAM: Think, Lindy, Lindy...do the authentically hip and happening spend alternate Friday nights in Turtle Bay discussing Philip Roth with dentists and shrinks? No, they party, and club, and Hamptonise with all the other shiney Now People.

LINDY: You were looking for clients. Networking. You said.

ADAM: I was. Till you came along.

LINDY: Well – thank you for trying to put me at ease.
You're very sweet. And tactful. You could have taught
your staff a thing or two.

ADAM: *My* staff?

LINDY: I imagine you're too upscale for body rings and
tattoos any more. Is that guy with the green off-center
Mohawk still there? And the GI Jane with engineer
boots and the big silver safety pin through her cheek?

ADAM: (*Laughs.*) Danika and Majjid! No, they disappeared
one day. With all the office computers.

LINDY: The place looked like a high-end drug rehab
center, that place. I expected a few Oxford shirts – a
turtle neck, maybe. I even dressed for the occasion –
Donna-Karen-casual.

ADAM: Wait. When were you in my office? In daylight, I
mean?

He has caught her.

LINDY: (*Shy.*) Once. Only the one time.

ADAM: (*Very curious.*) Which time; you never mentioned –

LINDY: It was a spur-of-the-moment thing.

ADAM: Oh?

LINDY: (*Torn between reticence and confession.*) I had a lunch
downtown… I thought, if you had a free moment, we
might –

ADAM: We might – ?

LINDY: You know, go for coffee, a drink. I sat there on the
futon. A pretty bizarre experience in daylight. And

clothed. Not to mention vertical. Watching your staff at work. So focused and self-assured, even the bizarros.

ADAM: Why didn't you wait for me?

LINDY: I felt... *exposed.*

ADAM: No one in the office knew about us. They probably took you for a client, a friend –

LINDY: But *I* knew what I was; a confused woman about to leave her husband. Which would mean her children, too, since the Metz Clan would move legal mountains to win custody of the little Bicycle Heirs.

ADAM: (*Trying to work it out.*) You dropped by my office – for a coffee – because you were thinking of leaving your husband?

LINDY: I was testing the water, seeing how it felt to be on the brink of giving up everything for New York, for writing – for you. But I felt trivial finally, watching your colleagues, all these driven people with real skills, with training and ambition. All I had, it suddenly struck me, was some vague dream of being a poet. And a bizarre notion that I could throw myself on the mercy of a man I barely knew.

ADAM: I was in love with you.

It hits her like an electric shock.

LINDY: (*Trying for calm.*) Surprise, surprise.

ADAM: I thought you had this ultra sensitive thing with my moods. How could you miss *that?*

LINDY: If you'd given the smallest sign…

ADAM: If.

LINDY: If, if, who knows what might have – / It's a long time ago.

ADAM: Except while the needle's back on the record –
what about now?

LINDY: Now *tonight*?

ADAM takes a moment to get this out.

ADAM: *Now*, ten years later.

LINDY: I'm lost. What are you asking?

ADAM is careful in saying this.

ADAM: Could I see you? When I'm out here?

LINDY: After what just happened?

ADAM: It doesn't have to be sex. I'd like to get re-
acquainted. That doesn't sound right – we never ended it,
did we…

LINDY: That's why we're here.

ADAM: To *end* it? I see. You planned this as a farewell
fuck?

LINDY: I wouldn't put it so elliptically. But, okay. When
you called it occurred to me the problem was, we never
ended it. People do, usually, don't they? Have a last time
together, *knowing* it's the last time. Doing whatever
people do; get sad, cry, feel each other slipping away…
Something about closure.

ADAM: But you don't want to make love. So what does that
leave? Say goodbye and no sex? Or spend the rest of the
night talking – and the rest of our lives wondering what
we missed?

LINDY: I didn't have a Plan B.

ADAM: (*Carefully.*) I do. Actually, it was closer to a long
term Plan A.

LINDY: (*Smiles, curious.*) Oh?

ADAM: (*On the spot.*) Do you have the key to that bar thing?

LINDY: It's open.

ADAM: (*Crossing to the bar.*) Can I get you something?

LINDY: (*Sing-song.*) Plan A?

ADAM finds a miniature scotch bottle in the 'bar'.

ADAM: Do you happen to remember a Friday after I think it was 'Madame Bovary'…?

LINDY: (*Smiling.*) 'Bright Lights, Big City'.

ADAM: Yes! (*Then.*) You know what I'm talking about?

LINDY: Of course.

ADAM: (*Unscrews the bottle.*) Well?

LINDY: (*Mocking.*) Well!?

He downs the tiny bottle, opens another.

ADAM: Were you…at all serious? Because *I* was.

LINDY: At the time, yes. In that way lovers are, when they say those things.

ADAM: I wasn't aware we were so statistically average.

LINDY: Isn't that the point of an affair, to make something ordinary feel like the first time ever?

ADAM: It was more than that. We vowed we'd always have each other while the rest of our life went on. It was a marriage, Lindy. A secret marriage.

LINDY: Yes, that was sweet.

ADAM: I've thought a lot about that idea over the years. More and more in fact. What a good thing it might have been –

LINDY: Another fairy tale.

ADAM: No, I've *seen* it. My partner's dad comes to town on business a couple three times a year and once up in Riverdale way off the beaten path, inspecting a job site, I saw him go into a restaurant with his arm around this plump smiley white haired lady with pink cheeks, you know, wire rim glasses, one of those jolly-sexy older liberal lady types. Herman turned and saw me. He's married, you see. I know his wife. She's great. They're a total family-family. My partner still thinks growing up with them ruined his chances for marriage because he'll never be as happy with someone as his folks are with each other, and it's true, they're happy. But there's his old dad – oh, right; six months later he treated our office to dinner, he's in town *with his wife* this time, and when I go in the men's room he's right behind me, boom, to the next stall. 'The woman you saw me with, we've been lovers for thirty-seven years. No one knows, not even my kid, you got that?' and he walks out. I found him back at the table with his arm around his wife…he loves her, too. Herman is an ordinary guy. Husband, provider – solid citizen. It's *not* a fairy tale.

LINDY: (*Studying him, then finally.*) No.

ADAM: I want you back.

LINDY: No, Adam.

ADAM: Why not?

LINDY: I can't even handle a casual night.

ADAM: A casual *farewell* night. This is different –

LINDY: Adam, you don't know…you can't begin to imagine how on the edge / I was *lost* after New York. Do you understand? Not immediately, not *right* after, but… (*Thinks back.*) Actually it was just a *sadness* at first, very slight. Which I took to be…the lack of a lover. I'd never had one before you, so I didn't know the signs. And I figured, okay, maybe what I need is someone to replace you, and practical-minded Lindy that I am, I found, *chose* actually, with cold-blooded calculation – poor man – the Curator of the Plains Indian Museum. I'm on the board, so no eyebrows rose over the odd meeting. And he was discrete, attentive…a thoroughly adequate choice, except for his aftershave, which smelled like banana. Not an erotic scent, I discovered. The problem was, nothing about him felt *necessary*. And this vague sadness inside, it was still there. So I ended it one day. Very cordial, *'Au revoir,* thanks for the sex, see you at the next board meeting.' Then out in the parking lot I started towards my car and…collapsed. Fell down in the snow desolate. Thinking of you. Buried under this tidal wave of grief.

ADAM doesn't know how to comfort her.

And with a family to manage. I had to schedule suffering between dishes and laundry. God save anyone from going through what I had to getting over you – without letting it show. Waking the kids. Making breakfast, packing lunch, getting them off to school in time to drive somewhere alone and lie down behind the steering wheel sobbing. Making love to your husband when every inch of you feels numb. Watching him move over you, and collapse, and you feel nothing at all.

She faces him now.

I'll never put myself through that again.

ADAM: You won't have to. (*Showing his beeper.*) I'm a beeper away. We can talk any time.

LINDY: No, Adam. Tonight settled one thing. It's all or nothing with us. And since it can't be all…

ADAM rises, walks around agitated, lost.

43

ADAM: How the hell did we get here so fast? I had this whole thing worked out to happen over months, we'd get to know each other and if all went well, okay, maybe we'd…reconnect fully after half a year at least, certainly that long before a night like – You're right, we *do* snowball.

She finds her glass.

LINDY: Speaking of which, my ice is melted.

ADAM: Lindy, we should say good night.

LINDY: (*A little too fast.*) Now?

ADAM: Let's give ourselves breathing room, time to cool off. Now that we know what happens with us, still – we could have a good night's sleep, let all this sink in. Decide how we feel about – seeing more of each other. And how much more. Then… I'll call you in the morning and see if you'd still like to have breakfast with me. How does that sound?

LINDY: (*Disappointed.*) Deeply responsible.

ADAM: And then, if the morning goes well / a step at a time.

LINDY: Let's not plan beyond breakfast.

ADAM: Breakfast. Sure.

LINDY: Eight – ish?

ADAM: (*Stalling.*) Don't you want to sleep late? Sunday?

LINDY: Trained by kids. Six-thirty, boi-oy-oy-oing, eyes open, hit the ground running.

ADAM: (*He smiles.*) I'll jog, I'll shower, then I'll call. (*Straightens hair with fingers.*) Eight-fifteen.

LINDY: (*Wryly.*) You jog?

ADAM: At my age it takes work to keep in shape.

LINDY: And whom for in-this-shape-do-we-keep?

ADAM: You're wicked, Lindy. Thanks for – for dinner.

LINDY: My pleasure. (*Thinks.*) Entirely, I'm afraid. (*Peering out into the hall.*) All clear.

ADAM: Would you mind – a quick goodnight kiss.

LINDY: A quick one.

They kiss lightly, but too long, her hands open by her side.

ADAM: Good night, Lindy.

LINDY: Good night, Adam.

ADAM stands close. Neither moves.

The lights fade.

End of Act One.

ACT TWO

Scene 1

Later.

LINDY and ADAM lie in bed, entangled, the covers bunched and gathered around them concealing much, but not all, of their naked bodies.

The food trolley remains, their half-eaten meal as we last saw it. Clothes lie everywhere.

Silence. Breathing. Stillness. Then –

LINDY: I have bad news.

ADAM: No!

LINDY: My leg.

ADAM: Don't say it.

LINDY: Asleep. Sorry.

ADAM: Alright, alright. Fast or slow?

LINDY: Medium.

ADAM: On a count of three?

BOTH: *One…two…three!*

> *LINDY pulls back her hips with a shudder of pleasure/pain.*

LINDY: I *hate* this part.

> *She sits up kneading her leg.*

ADAM: *You* hate it!? I'm the one out here in the cold, all shrivelled and sad.

LINDY: They're such funny little things. Like a furry animal with a life all its own.

ADAM: The image isn't helpful right now.

LINDY: I wonder what it would be like to have one of my own?

ADAM: You'd be a morphadike.

LINDY: Morphadike?

ADAM: Roo's word. They did earthworms in science. He couldn't believe two sexes in the same body.

LINDY: Ahhh, 'morphadike'. Nice.

ADAM: I asked if he knew what made men and women different. 'Males go out and you see everything, females go in so you have to guess.' That's what he said.

LINDY: I like this boy.

ADAM: Me, too. A lot.

LINDY rises wrapping a sheet around her.

Why the sheet?

LINDY: At our age, modesty is advised. Out of bed, anyway.

She stands and takes a step, wobbling.

ADAM: Still asleep?

LINDY: That ain't sleep, darlin', it's Wobbly Knees, the Push Button Cow. Feeling extremely moo.

She chuckles while hobbling around to get circulation back in her legs.

How did we manage this every other Friday? Where did we find the energy?

She sits at the table, smiling, basking.

ADAM: We rise to the occasion.

LINDY: Bliss. Utter…complete…obscene…perfect bliss. I
   bet we're the only guests awake right now. Maybe in the
   whole state. What if we were the last people on earth?
   Would that be nice, would you like that, Adam?

ADAM is silent.

ADAM?!

ADAM: (*Startled awake.*) Hello?

LINDY: Don't you dare fall asleep on me.

ADAM: (*Dreamily.*) I was checking my eyelids for holes.

LINDY: All you men want to do is doze off afterwards.
   Honestly!

She's idly picking food from plates, nibbling.

ADAM: And what do 'you *women*' want to do…*afterwards*?

LINDY: Talk, dance, fight a war!

ADAM: You'd win, no contest. Just get all the women in the
   world to put out for all the guys at once and when they
   fall asleep afterwards, kill 'em.

LINDY starts cutting her steak into squares.

LINDY: I wrote some poems about us.

ADAM takes a moment to hear this, then props himself up.

She speaks his imaginary reaction.

'Oh, God, she's going to read to me, I have to listen and
pretend it's good, is this the price of sex?!' Don't worry, I
didn't bring little 'Jock and Julienne' with me; that's the
title. Isn't it *awful!* Nursery rhymes, kind of, about this
little boy and girl lost in a fairytale city. Very erotic.

ADAM: I'd like to read them.

LINDY: No.

ADAM: One day?

LINDY: I want you to know they exist is all. That you were in my thoughts. A lot. Next topic.

She doesn't look at him, but slices with renewed concentration.

ADAM: You seem to be controlling this situation.

LINDY: (*Smiling.*) That's cause I have a knife.

ADAM: What are you doing over there, Lindy Metz?

LINDY: Cutting red meat into bite sized chunks. Energy for the night ahead.

ADAM: (*Mock horror.*) More!? She wants *more!?*

LINDY: I'm stocking up. Winters out here can be long and cold.

ADAM: We have all tomorrow. And…after. Don't we?

He sits now, looks at her.

Pause.

LINDY: (*Finally, she says.*) *And* we have tonight!

She carries the plate to the bed, sits cross legged and places a cube of meat in her mouth, licking her fingers.

Mmmmmm.

She takes another cube of meat and holds it out.

He sucks it into his mouth.

ADAM: You know how I want to spend tomorrow? Actually, it's today already…later today? I want to go swimming. The hotel guide mentioned granite quarries a few miles out of town…

LINDY: You don't want to see me in a bathing suit, you really don't.

ADAM: Haven't I seen everything already?

LINDY: (*With a brief odd look.*) Not by a very long shot.

ADAM: Well at least you're embarrassed. Which means you're thinking about it. That was a trick question to see if you were serious about tomorrow.

She eats a cube, then feeds him.

Thank you.

LINDY: I like feeding you; you put something in me, I put something in you. 'Oh, mom, you are sooo deep,' that's what Doug says when I spin off into one of my little brain-travel things –

ADAM averts his face suddenly and pulls on his boxer shorts.

What's the matter? Adam?

He turns his back to her.

Is it something I said?

ADAM: No. Give me a second. (*Controlling deep emotion.*) I'm not used to being fussed over – / Sorry.

LINDY: A little roast beef goes a long way with you. I'll have to remember that.

ADAM ignores her attempt to lighten things.

ADAM: Even the smallest things you do, the Goofy Gifts –

LINDY: Any excuse to shop, darlin'.

ADAM: Do you do that for Hugh? Study him, figure out what he'd like?

LINDY: (*Trying to lighten things.*) More roast beef?

She feeds him another cube.

ADAM: Amazing. Melinda Metz. There were times I thought I might have made you up. Sometimes at work designing a room I picture the two of us in it wandering around, having dinner, making love. My staff thinks I'm having creative brainstorms. I'm with you, that's all. Even in the morning while I jog, I imagine you running alongside –

LINDY: *Jogging!?* Me?!! Please, adultery's one thing but I draw the line at exercise.

ADAM: (*Playing along.*) All right, you sleep late, I'll bring home a coffee from Starbucks after my run.

LINDY: That's better, darling. Keep it light and sweet, like my coffee, three sugars. And a chocolate eclair, wouldn't you *die* for a chocolate eclair right now, or one of those strawberries dipped in chocolate, chocolate *anything*, was there any chocolate in the bar?

She crosses the room and searches the 'bar'.

ADAM resumes his previous thought.

ADAM: In the evening, putting Roo to bed, I imagine you across the room watching me from beside the hamster cage while I horse around tucking him in. A sort of secret friend who sees me being a good father –

LINDY: God, look at all these ways to get fat.

ADAM: Family's all I ever really wanted. Success always seemed easy, but to make a family. And hold it together. I'm embarrassed how much I love being in my house, just…being there, with my kid, everything snug and safe. I'd picture someone in my life to share that with.

LINDY: Macadamia nuts?

ADAM: Anyway, the thought of you got me through some pretty bleak nights, and I promised myself, if I ever saw you again, and found the right moment, I'd thank you.

LINDY: (*Discovers.*) M&Ms!

ADAM: One more thing –

LINDY: I get the point, Adam. You're welcome for whatever you think I helped you get through.

ADAM: There's so many things we never said in the New York days.

LINDY: Couldn't we just be quiet and eat chocolate together?

ADAM: Are feelings still a forbidden topic?

LINDY: I don't want the past dragged into… *now.* Or the future. Just let's be – quiet. Okay? If you knew how much it means to me to feel this serene. To know it's still possible…

ADAM doesn't fully understand her meaning, but he senses her need.

ADAM: Then promise me we'll spend tomorrow together.

LINDY: That's too far away, I can't picture it.

ADAM: Lindy!

LINDY: Shhh. Eat something. Chocolate. Steak. Get your strength back.

ADAM: (*Suddenly challenging.*) So we can fuck a few more times before you vanish? For good this time?

LINDY: I guess I can kiss this little calm of mine goodbye.

ADAM: That's the plan, isn't it? Rut and revel till dawn then 'Adios, Sunshine'? How do I know you'll be here when I wake up?

LINDY: (*Sharp.*) How do I know you have a client in town?

ADAM: What?

LINDY: You could have made him up for all I know. You could have made up the whole job out here.

ADAM: You think I'm crazy?

LINDY: How could I think anything, I barely *know* you! And you certainly don't know me! If you want to picture me as some kind of nourishing earth-mother type lurking in your kid's bedroom watching you play daddy, fine, but don't feel you have to share it with me because all it does is make me wonder what desperate situation sent you chasing out here in the first place –

She is agitated now, and annoyed.

Why did you have to start?! It was perfect a moment ago!

ADAM: It was perfect ten years ago.

LINDY: It was exactly *not* perfect or we'd have been able to say the simple things to each other like 'I love you. Be with me. Let's find a way'. All we did was hide behind feverish talk about books, then fuck and fuck for hours on end.

She stops herself, forcing calm to return.

ADAM: Let's not make that same mistake again.

LINDY: Oh for pity's sake, Adam, what's wrong, just spit it out? Did you leave your wife? Are you *thinking* of leaving her? Did you just learn you have a fatal illness and I'm your last hurrah?

They exchange a look, then explode with laughter.

ADAM: I'm in perfect health. And my marriage is – completely functional.

LINDY: Then what's this all about?

ADAM: I told you –

LINDY: No, no, Adam, you're here because of *me*, right? This job is because of me.

ADAM: Yes and no.

LINDY: Mainly yes.

ADAM: I've known where you were for a few years. I spend a lot of time on-line these days with Jan on the road. I started searching the Web for old school mates, girl friends – One day, there you were. I didn't dare call…till this job happened.

LINDY: You see how this puts a certain *pressure* on me? I do have a life, you know.

ADAM: We both do.

LINDY: I don't want this.

ADAM: I don't believe you.

LINDY: You know so little about me.

ADAM: I know you came to my office one day to change your life. I know you made yourself free tomorrow in case seeing me again stirred things – Okay, it's scary for both of us, so we made up excuses for tonight. 'I'm here for a job.' Not only a good reason to come, but if the you-and-me part of the trip doesn't work out, I still come home with work. But *your* ploy, much more cunning; a farewell night. There I'll be lying next to you afterwards with all your scents on me, the feel of your body, your breath in my ear, knowing I'll lose it all for good if I don't make a move, show my hand. And once you've seen it you can play your cards…if you decide to. Am I warm? Hot?

ADAM, without pre-planning his tirade, has blundered his way to the truth.

LINDY: (*Pause.*) Scalding.

ADAM: You're a coward.

LINDY: Just cautious. I think ahead. What if the night with you had turned out –

ADAM: Awful?

LINDY: The opposite. If it turned out like this.

They at last approach each other with the full terror and respect their attraction warrants. They kiss and quickly entangle, desire flaring like a struck match. They stagger towards the bed. She forces herself to stop, now on edge.

Aren't we too old?

ADAM: *Way* too old.

LINDY: How do we even go about it? I've forgotten the rules!

ADAM: To hell with rules.

LINDY: Oh, Adam, rules are everything; what, when, where, how often?

ADAM: We didn't need them in New York.

LINDY: You're so wrong. From the minute we saw each other at – Dr Gasarch's?

ADAM: Hecht. The dermatologist. That's where we met.

LINDY: (*Animated.*) 'Crime and Punishment', I remember. I never had it come to me so distinctly that I was going to sleep with a man. After that, the whole discussion was about us, about the transgression ahead, the idea of it. 'Crime and Punishment'. God what a sexy night.

ADAM: (*Remembering.*) Yeah.

LINDY: Then the rules began. 'Avoid his eyes.' 'Cover your tracks.' 'Don't look at him.' 'Leave separately.' 'Disagree with him about the odd book, he says Gravity's Rainbow is groundbreaking, argue that it's incomprehensible.'

ADAM: You want to know the truth? I never read it.

LINDY: No one *read* the books, Adam. Except you and me, the others came for the food. And I came to show off – to flirt. To make love.

ADAM: (*Then.*) Fine; we'll make rules.

LINDY: Are you a good liar?

ADAM: (*Not expecting this.*) What kind of question is that?

LINDY: We're putting our families in each other's hands. Can you lie for all of us? 'Cause if we get careless, or desperate, and spill our heart to the person nearest at hand – remember 'Crime and Punishment', the guilty need to confess more than they fear punishment. That's Fyodor, hon, not Melinda. There's three young lives that could get run over by accident if our little deception gets away from us.

ADAM: You can trust me.

LINDY: What'll you tell Jan when you travel?

LINDY is strangely energised, beyond mischievous. She watches ADAM like a scientist studying an animal.

ADAM: 'I'm away on business.'

LINDY: (*As ADAM's wife.*) 'To see *that woman*?' (*As LINDY.*) I'm being your wife. She'll figure out what's going on sooner or later, and she'll wait until you're off guard then ambush you from behind the coffee pot. How do you answer her?

LINDY's force is relentless, irresistible.

ADAM: She'll never notice.

LINDY: She's human, Adam, she's a woman.

ADAM: She's busy with other things.

LINDY: You mean work? Don't let that fool you. Women feel everything, even if we don't say a word – in fact *especially* then, because silence is the ultimate weapon. (*With growing animation.*) Can you stand up to complete isolation, the way only a woman hurting badly knows how to isolate her beloved; smiles and touches with no feeling behind them excpet silent rage, can you keep your nerve through that?

ADAM: What happened to that serene mood you were in?

She starts popping M&Ms into her mouth rapidly, speaking while she chews.

LINDY: Maybe you're already at war and don't even know it. If she smells that you were never hers to begin with, anything's possible – her career could be revenge on you for waiting nine-ish years to propose. A woman can forgive almost anything except hesitation in desiring her and my God, after making her wait that long you may have reached a point where the only decent thing left to do was walk away.

ADAM: I did.

LINDY's animation unnerves ADAM.

He feels raw and de-stabilised.

LINDY: You did *what?*

ADAM: I left Jan.

LINDY: No, Adam. Please don't say you're here because –

ADAM: (*Growing agitated.*) Not *tonight*, for God sake. *Before.* In New York. I mean, I packed…stored a suitcase in a closet at the office. I wrote long notes to myself about how I'd ask you to live with me. Leave your husband, write full time – my mind was back and forth for weeks, one minute thinking you'd laugh at me for being some downtown freak who totally missed the signals, and the next minute I'd think, no, she's unhappy, never talks about her life, if I take her off guard with a dramatic gesture… So I decided finally to risk it.

LINDY: And you got cold feet. Oo-blah-dee.

ADAM: I planned it for the next Book Circle. You weren't there. You missed the next one, too. And the one after.

LINDY: Wait a minute. You don't mean…?

ADAM: You'd left New York.

LINDY: Oh, Adam, that's just the saddest thing I ever heard. One Friday later and we might have –

ADAM: Who knows. Maybe I'd have got cold feet.

LINDY: Did you really mean to / you're not just saying it to make me feel less like an idiot for…having had ideas?

ADAM: I got home that night, Jan was standing at the stove naked, drenched in sweat, 11:30 pm, cooking chili. So out of character. I thought, 'Who is this stranger I've been living with for ten years?' The way she watched me come through the door, the fury in her eyes – not *just* fury; need, desperation. It just came out of me, this thing I'd never said, never been able to say before. 'I love you.'

LINDY is still, M&Ms in her lap.

LINDY: In ten years you never…?

ADAM: Neither of us. We didn't – *say* those things. But that night something changed for a moment. We were naked, in a trance, no, more a physical *place* – (*Thinks.*) Paradise, really.

LINDY: Another fairy tale.

ADAM: She got pregnant that night. We didn't know when she left the next day – dance tour in Yugoslavia. She never called. Never wrote, not once in two months. And she came back different; guarded, distant –

LINDY: Why?

ADAM: (*With effort.*) Time was running out. You see, she didn't want children. Never had. Two months gone, a choice had to be made –

LINDY: (*Understanding.*) Oh, dear.

ADAM: And I won. But the cost... It was a terrible pregnancy, three months in bed on her back. All that physical agony for something she didn't even want. She basically threw away her career for me –

LINDY: Her choice –

ADAM: But *for me*, she did it because *I* wanted a child, because I thought, I told myself she'll change with motherhood, soften, relax inside. As if a child might change her into more the kind of woman she was that one night and I could love her again.

LINDY: Was it good as us?

ADAM: Ridiculous, right? To think a trip here could solve anything. I'm in the wrong life.

LINDY: Then leave.

ADAM: Not possible.

LINDY: You already did once – almost.

ADAM: Before certain vows were made.

LINDY: Marriage vows are negotiable.

ADAM: To Roo. To my son. His friend's family went through an ugly divorce and now he's terrified the same thing'll happen to / he feels the chill in our house. He made me swear on his life I'd never leave his mom.

He's watching her, baffled suddenly.

LINDY: Oh, Adam, you didn't!

ADAM: (*Feeling totally exposed.*) Talking to you feels more like betrayal than making love, why is that?

LINDY: Words are personal. Sex is just – bodies.

He stands, now resolute, precise.

ADAM: Here's what I've decided; I need intimacy. I can't find it with my wife. So either I forget that need, or I find a woman I can be close to. And I've decided on the latter.

LINDY: (*Laughing.*) Am I a finalist, or was this the first cut?

ADAM: That didn't come out right. What I mean is, don't feel pressured. I'd like it to be you, but – if you're worried I'm not a good enough liar…

LINDY: Poor darling, I was mouthing off, you're not supposed to listen when I get like that.

ADAM: I'm sorry to dump all this on you.

LINDY: (*Quieter.*) It's just…bad timing.

ADAM: I meant to slip this idea in gradually.

LINDY: I'm flattered by your loss of control. But Hugo needs me right now. Badly. He ran the business into the ground. We're bankrupt.

ADAM: Jesus.

LINDY: We'll hardly end up in the Poor House, darling. But he'll need my undivided attention during his run for the Senate. Thank God for politics to fall back on when all else fails. Stop, Lindy. That's so damned unfair. I am, though; unfair, demanding, temperamental. He deserved someone lower maintenance.

ADAM: What a mess.

LINDY: Poor Hugo, so patient and forgiving – so unbearably fucking forgiving. Why should I need forgiveness? I don't forgive *him* for failing. (*Stops.*) Oh, dear, I said it. He's a failure. My husband is a failure. He failed in New York, he failed out here. I'm sorry, Adam, but you see what a bitch you lust after?

She wanders in circles, wiping off objects, trying to tidy her surroundings.

ADAM: You're upset, who wouldn't be –

LINDY: Don't be insightful and sympathetic; we're *talking* now. God I envy your wife. She married a success. She's the choice of a man who *succeeds!* Whereas I, who chose security, I end up the door prize of a great big zero with pedigree. You know what I actually had in mind tonight, if you showed up here all middle aged and puffy, I thought I might put the moves on you while I still have allure – which I do, I'm well aware, God knows I work hard enough at it –

ADAM: You were planning to seduce me from Jan?

LINDY: I am that small.

ADAM: Go for it.

LINDY: (*Suddenly quiet.*) Not in the cards, darlin'. The most we can hope for is nights like this.

ADAM: Nights? That's plural. Are more nights in store? Is it official, we're having an affair?

She gazes at him, mesmerised. A faint twerbling noise, the cell-phone in her purse. She doesn't respond.

Lindy?

LINDY: (*Abstracted.*) Do you hear something?

ADAM: Your phone.

LINDY: (*Coming to.*) But I held my calls – (*Thinks, realises it's.*) Cell-phone! Keeshon! Oh Lord, I have to take this…

LINDY seems distracted, as if she forgot where phones are kept.

ADAM: In your handbag.

LINDY: How do I sound, is my voice normal?

She examines her face closely, squinting in the mirror.

My pupils get huge sometimes, that's another sign, how big are they, I can't see them?

ADAM: Lindy, what's going on?

LINDY: (*Chants encouragement to herself, only half aware of ADAM.*) I need to be strong for him, we live up to each other, that's our deal.

She has taken the phone out. She answers.

Hello?

She looks quickly at ADAM.

Oh. / Hi. / No, Hugh, I was asleep. (*Fake yawn.*) / Yes, I know my phone was off / What is this, the third degree? / Why this checking up on me at three in the morning? / You can't what? / Oh, poor poopie.

She talks with increasing speed and animation, soaring with her own words.

Wait, hold that thought. 'I can't sleep because you're not with me and I miss you.' That's so sweet, darling, but the thing is, when I *am* home you can't sleep either, but we've somehow shifted the blame for this insomnia to your anxiety about the kids having nightmares, meaning of course 'nightmares about the unstable element in their lives; Mom!' And all this emotional drain leaves him too exhausted to focus on his business affairs, do I have that about right?

She becomes wittily pedantic, the absolute life of the party.

So my question to you would have to be; With Mrs Cross-to-Bear out of the picture shouldn't you sleep better, not worse? Or is this one of those oh so familiar damned-if-I-do-damned-if-I-don't scenarios whereby I'm a millstone round your neck no matter what the fuck I do at home or away, darling – (*She stops, listens.*) … Hugh?

Now she looks worried.

(*Screams.*) Hugh!?

She hangs up.

ADAM watches her.

Was that a little zig-zaggy? I can get zig-zaggy.

ADAM: You better tell me what's happening, Lindy.

LINDY: I knew the calm was too good to last. There was a time I could fly level for months at a time without chemicals.

Roots in her handbag, speaking faster.

This launch feels pretty smooth, relative to some I could name, like the infamous lawn party / when we moved out here to Hugoland. Before his family met me / well, refused to in fact, cause Hugh hadn't first run his bride

past the Metz Genetic Quality Control Committee. I
wanted to rub their noses in chic, Mama Metz and all her
lumbering Country Club Tutons; My legendary Black
and White Party, oh, Adam, you should have seen it;
dance band, tent, even the food; pasta with white sauce
and black truffles, God it was swank. Not even a freak
thunderstorm could blunt the high spirits. It flattened the
entire tent, and everyone went racing into the
conservatory, but Unflappable Lindy strode forth chin
high into the storm and proceeded to re-raise the tent.
What could they do but follow me laughing into the
downpour, tra-la. Only, when I looked up from wrestling
a tentpole, there they were, motionless silhouettes behind
the conservatory windows watching me outside in the
rain, raving. Tra-la!

She stops, takes some pills from her handbag.

ADAM: Jesus!

LINDY: What a way for poor Hugh to learn his vivacious-
if-sometimes-moody young bride and mother of the
bicycle babies was 'chemically challenged'. (*Off his look.*)
Manic depressive. In the bi-polar sense. (*Beat.*) He's been
very good about it. Considering I never told him. (*Beat.*)
He wouldn't have married me, you see. (*Jiggling the pill
bottle.*) Water?

ADAM gets one a glass and hands it to her on the bed.

ADAM: It's warm. (*Of the pills.*) What are those?

LINDY: Squeezies, I call them. We have pet names for the
meds, all us ladies of the Bi-Polaroid Society, our
support group. Zonkers. Hammers. Whatever sends you
back to the D.G.N., the old Dull Gray Nothing, sort of
like TV with the sound off. Life without the awful peaks
and valleys. Alas, no orgasm, either. Which is why, for
gala moments – for *you* – heigh-ho, heigh-ho, it's off the

pills we go. And the cow flies over the moon, straight into orbit sometimes. Sorry you had to see this.

She pops pills and drinks some water.

They'll kick in by tomorrow. Just taking them helps – psychothingamally.

She smiles.

ADAM: Better?

LINDY: Shall we move on to what you'll find listed in your program as the second-thoughts portion of tonight's entertainment.

ADAM: Second thoughts? (*Smirks.*) Oh. Was this supposed to scare me away?

LINDY: It damn well should.

ADAM: Hence the one-night-stand? So I'd never learn the horrible truth?

LINDY: Oh, Adam, that was nothing. When I truly launch… I've been known to staple the curtains together and crawl under the rug shrieking like a banshee.

ADAM: What if I told you I didn't care.

LINDY: I'd say you were taking gallantry to surreal excess.

ADAM: Gallantry has nothing to do with it.

LINDY: Are you *kinky*, Adam?

ADAM: Why should I care one way or another? I don't have to bring the bad stuff home with me, it's not my problem, is it?

LINDY: (*Pause.*) That would be, what, extreme tact disguised as callous indifference?

ADAM: We'll only have the best of each other. No dirty
laundry.

LINDY: I'd wear you down, lover. When I met my husband,
he never drank. Steady as an ocean liner, one speed
Hugo. Now –

ADAM: (*Approaching her tenderly.*) Come here.

LINDY: (*Vulnerable.*) How can I talk you out of this?

ADAM embraces her.

ADAM: Too late.

LINDY: Lie with me. Hold me for the time we have left.

*As ADAM leads her to the bed the alarm/radio snaps on at
top volume, shattering the silence.*

LINDY leaps up.

ADAM fumbles with the unit.

*LINDY acts shocked, electrified. She bumps to the music, with
increasing wildness.*

LET IT PLAY!!!

She dances over and turns the radio back up.

ADAM: Lindy, other guests…!!!

LINDY: Who cares!? I paid for this fucking room. Is there a
law against partying when you're in the mood, and oh
am I ever in the mood for once in God knows how many
centuries…

ADAM turns off the music.

Dance with me, sugar!

*She starts toward the alarm/radio to turn it up and ADAM
blocks her.*

You're afraid, aren't you. That's better, you're getting smart now.

ADAM: You want everyone to know you had a visitor?!

LINDY: 'It was bad enough when I thought I'd have to listen to *poetry* for God sake, now the dizzy bitch wants to *party*!'

She turns the volume up full.

Dance, baby, we only have an hour till he gets here.

ADAM: *Who?*

LINDY: My dear husband. He's coming to save Miss-Naughty-Wife. Didn't you hear my telltale loony-toon voice on the phone? He did. (*Talking louder and louder.*) He hears every ping in the drive chain. He even knows when I've skipped my meds so I can feel alive for a change –

She dances over and gets meat from her plate and feeds him.

Open wide, baby-baby. Let me feed you. Let me sit in a corner and watch you play Daddy-Waddy-kins. Come on, lover, eat my meat, get strong and warm and safe with me, Adam, please please God let someone in the world feel safe with me!

She's forcing him to eat. Her strength is unnatural.

ADAM: Lindy... I can't breathe.

He throws her back.

LINDY is stunned.

LINDY: Oh, shit – (*Shaking violently now.*) Grab me, hold my arms tight against my body.

ADAM: (*Embracing her from behind.*) I'm here.

LINDY: Get me in the shower, as hot as you can make it.

ADAM: (*Helping her.*) No problem, tell me what you need…

LINDY: (*At wit's end.*) There's so little of me missing. You can barely see it with a microscope. It's so fucking unfair. Don't leave me alone…

ADAM: (*Steering her to the bathroom.*) I'm here, Lindy. I won't go away. I'm right here. Right here.

They're in the bathroom.

Lights fade.

Scene 2

Later.

LINDY dozes in bed, propped on pillows, hair wet. ADAM sits vigil on a nearby chair, his hair also wet. Both wear fluffy white terrycloth robes with hotel coat-of-arms.

LINDY moves her head. Her eyes blink open. She sees ADAM watching her.

LINDY: (*Groggy.*) Hi.

ADAM: Better?

LINDY: How bad was it?

He waves the question away.

ADAM: What can I get you? Water? Cold coffee?

LINDY: You're good at this. It's not gone unnoticed.

ADAM: (*Checking his watch.*) Is it too early to order breakfast? I'm starving.

LINDY: (*Suddenly alert.*) Oh, Christ, Adam, you shouldn't be here, not now.

She notes the time, relaxes a little.

Fifteen minutes? I thought I slept – it felt like hours.

ADAM: I get the whole morning with you, you promised.

LINDY: Put your clothes on. We have to clean up the evidence (*Mind racing.*) – the Interstate at this hour – on Sunday! He could be here any minute.

ADAM: Who?

LINDY: My husband, I *told* you…

ADAM: I thought that was just part of the –

LINDY: Did he call back while I was asleep? If he's not sure I launched, he could phone back and double check before he saddles the horse.

ADAM: No calls.

LINDY: Then he's on his way. (*Realising.*) No calls??!! (*Eureka!*) Keeshon got through the night. Bravo.

ADAM: What'll you do when he arrives?

She lifts the cover off and swings heavy legs over the side of the bed.

LINDY: Don't worry, I'm an old hand at handling Der Hugo.

She rises and gets her balance.

Did I say anything unforgivable? I'm told I can get pretty brutal in full vent.

ADAM: I only remember the good parts.

LINDY: You're so full of it, Adam. Bless you.

ADAM: Are you more or less / back to –

LINDY: Normal, yes; *my* normal. You'd better get dressed.

She puts dishes on the trolley.

ADAM starts dressing.

An uneasy silence.

ADAM: About these rules of ours. Am I allowed to call your office? How much lead time do you need before I come out?

LINDY loads dishes, her mood remote.

LINDY: (*Finally.*) Let's not make this harder than it is.

ADAM: I'll be back in a few weeks. Three at the outside. I'll leave you my beeper number.

LINDY: (*A smile.*) Your *beeper!* Aren't we getting personal!

ADAM: So you can reach me if, in case, you know –

LINDY: I'm teasing. By all means, leave me your beeper.

ADAM stops dressing, alert to her tone.

ADAM: So…it's settled? We're lovers.

LINDY: Say goodbye, Adam.

ADAM: You can't change your mind again. I won't let you.

LINDY: Is that a threat? What'll you do, call my home and breathe into the answering machine?

ADAM: I could, you know.

LINDY's not sure this is a joke.

LINDY: I guess we're at each other's mercy now.

ADAM: I love you.

LINDY: But it costs you nothing, Adam. A phone call, a few lies, a plane ticket. For me every visit means two days off medication, plus all that self-monitoring while the pills wear down / watching for signs of lift-off…

ADAM: Why would every visit have to be all or nothing? We'll mix it up; some days for carnival, other times just a quiet weekend together – a little TV with the sound off –

She stops clearing the table for a moment and studies him.

LINDY: I don't need you for Dull Gray. I have Hugh for that.

ADAM: But only that. With us there's a choice. You can be wild as you want, dance, talk, eat chocolate, and at the end of the day, no dirty laundry.

LINDY: (*Chuckling.*) You are so *male.*

ADAM: I meant to speak for both of us.

LINDY: That's what a fantasy *is*, Adam, when you speak for all the people in it. When they start talking back it's called reality.

ADAM: Isn't this what you want?

LINDY: How long could it last, this place without dirty laundry? Think, darling. What if it keeps being wonderful? How long before the occasional weekend isn't enough and we start wondering why we can't spend a little more time together, then a little more, until finally we'd make something happen, not deliberately, just the way people do, a slip-up, evidence left lying around –

She sees a tie half under the bed and pulls it out; voila!

Or we'd get carried away and lose track of time – (*Noting the time.*) Jesus, Adam, get dressed!

ADAM starts to button his shirt, but grows frustrated.

ADAM: So that's how you talk yourself out of it.

LINDY: What?

ADAM: Everything you want –

LINDY: Careful, Adam –

ADAM: You stack up the problems till there's no way but out, and it feels so wise and prudent that you made the noble sacrifice and saved everyone from a terrible mess, God, what self-deluding crap. People go a whole life looking for what we have, and you're about to throw it away, like you threw poetry away, and New York, and me once upon time – because you're afraid to take a chance –

LINDY: I'm not afraid.

ADAM: Then what, what the hell is stopping you?

LINDY: I don't think you want to know.

ADAM: More surprises, wonderful!!!

LINDY: (*Carefully.*) Why did you come here?

ADAM: What part of 'I love you' don't you understand? You're everything I want.

LINDY once again watches him with unnerving intensity.

LINDY: For what?

ADAM: (*Baffled.*) To be with. To talk to. To love –

LINDY: – Honour and cherish? For richer or poorer? In sickness and in health?

She is smiling. Ah, a test!

ADAM: Poetically speaking.

LINDY: In prose, Adam.

ADAM: What are you getting at?

LINDY: This woman you imagine watching you put your kid to bed, making you feel understood – is this your idea of the perfect mistress? Cause it sounds to me more like the ideal wife.

ADAM: Wife?!

LINDY: You came to kick the tires, darling. To see if I measure up to your dream life, if I'd be someone to leave your marriage for?

ADAM: Whoa, where did 'marriage' come from?

LINDY: The same place where you hide everything you don't want to face. You're here to shop for a wife. How scared are you now you've seen the merchandise?

ADAM: I have no intention of leaving Jan.

LINDY: As long as I'm out here to ease the pressure.

ADAM: You're twisting this around.

LINDY: We're not two happy people looking for a now-and-then extramarital squeeze, like your partner's dad and his white haired bounce. You and me, we dream about something very different.

ADAM: (*Rallying.*) So, your 'episode' didn't put me off, time to haul out the M word, that's sure to send me running, then whose fault is it that nothing came of tonight?! Is that the game?

LINDY: *You* called *me*, darling.

ADAM: I'm not trying to escape my marriage.

LINDY: Too bad. Cause I am. Except I'm not afraid to call it by name. No, that's a lie, I'm terrified. Actually, yes, right now I'm more frightened than I've ever been.

ADAM: Did you plan this from the start?

LINDY: I've only felt complete surrender with one man. I let him get away once. But if I had a second chance –

ADAM: You'd leave Hugh?

LINDY comes close, slowly unbuttoning his mis-buttoned shirt, then rebuttoning it correctly, not meeting his eyes, only watching her fingers as she speaks.

LINDY: I'm numb from years of taking blame for his failures. My so-called condition's his excuse for everything he can't solve with a smile, a handshake and a high-fibre diet. I've been patient, God knows – while he ran his business into the ground through stubbornness and inattention, claiming I took all his attention when the simple truth is…I'm far stronger than him…than most people, in fact. Not much choice, with my chemistry you're either a train wreck, or – remarkable me. And I am, you know, a wonderful wife and mother, for one. My kids are smart and lovely and incredibly tough – not jock tough in the Metz tradition, but deep-inside strong, like their mother. Plus I'm a gifted teacher – my results have been called astonishing. True, I'm a terrible housekeeper. And I tend to put on weight, but I'm a disciplined dieter, plus a great cook and an awesome hostess. My nose turns red when I'm embarrassed. What else – oh, yes, I'm missing a tiny strand of protein in my DNA which renders me a little wobbly round the axis on occasion, but these are tiny flaws.

ADAM: What's going on here, Lindy?

LINDY: I'm buttoning your shirt.

ADAM: No, what are you…*saying?*

LINDY: Are you catching my jitters? Cause I'm catching your calm.

ADAM: Is this chemicals or something deliberate?

LINDY: I'm listing my qualification. On the whole I'm an amazing catch, and I'd like to spend what's left of my life with a man who appreciates me, and knows that 'different' isn't something to fear, since he went his own way and made a success of being different –

ADAM: I'm not afraid.

LINDY: Then why the affair-for-life? Why the promise to your son? Why all these tricks to keep distance between us. Intimacy takes courage. You can't put furniture in the doorway.

She pats his shirt and steps back.

(*Admiring the shirt.*) There, that's better.

ADAM: Lindy –

LINDY: It's not me who's afraid, Adam. It's you.

ADAM finally becomes worked up.

ADAM: (*Circling her.*) I don't believe this! Back in New York you're too frightened to call and say goodbye, and now after one night together –

LINDY: – One night and ten years –

ADAM: Don't get clever. You'd never leave your husband, your kids, just like that –

LINDY: (*Rueful.*) If you say so.

ADAM: It's just…not like you.

LINDY: One more of the many things you don't know about me.

ADAM: You'd leave your whole life behind and –

LINDY: I'd marry you. And make a home for us. And take care of you in the best tradition of a good Cranbrook Junior, every vase with well chosen flowers. Maybe one day introduce you to my children, and hope they'd learn from a man who'd made something of his life. Maybe even get to know your son in time – all that messy stuff. With luck we'd grow old together. I'd die one minute after you so you'd never be alone, and I'd have no time for a broken heart. You see, you're not the only one with embarrassing fantasies.

ADAM: But would you *do* it. If I said pack your bag right now –

LINDY: Say it. I dare you.

ADAM: How did we get to this?

LINDY: (*Sure he's wriggling out.*) Have you forgotten anything; socks, wallet, credit card?

ADAM: Dry your hair, get dressed, pack. Come with me. Now.

LINDY: Careful, Adam. For a moment I almost believed you.

ADAM: We'll rent a car, drive somewhere, figure out the next step...

LINDY: Adam, for God sake, think what you're saying.

ADAM: I've spent my whole life thinking / thinking and analysing / weighing the options, and by the time I decide what to do it's either wrong, or I'm too late. I want you, Lindy. It's why I'm here, you're right. I want you.

LINDY: I appreciate the ardour –

ADAM: No more slipaway tricks.

LINDY: I'm talking about practical things –

ADAM: I'm talking about everything else. I wish you were whole and perfect, I wish I hadn't made a mess of my personal life, and I'm scared shitless, I mean this could be the biggest mistake I'll ever make, but I don't care. I want you.

LINDY: This is so very dangerous.

ADAM: Tell me anything worth doing that couldn't potentially fuck up your whole life.

LINDY: Alright, Adam. Alright.

ADAM: You'll come?

LINDY: Yes. (*Reeling.*) I'll get dressed –

ADAM: Throw on a coat, no one'll see at this hour –

LINDY: I can't sneak away like that, naked under a coat!?

ADAM: Why not…like old times.

LINDY: (*It starts to sink in.*) But it's not, it's not old times, we can't undo what we do now. We need some time.

ADAM: For what?

LINDY: Oh, you know; everything. To make arrangements, explain, I have Hugh, the boys; you have Greg, it's only fair.

ADAM: No. You'll get scared and bargain away the chance. I know this game. 'It can't be real!' 'It won't last.' Who'd really want someone like me when they knew my secrets, right? So we jump on the first train that passes. That's how you ended up with Hugh, and me with Jan, we never chose, we settled, and ever since it's been about – yeah, you're right, rules, but the wrong rules. Being responsible, mature, doing the right thing. Self-righteous cowards, that's us, knowing our life doesn't work but too afraid to put it right because…why? We might upset all the people making us unhappy to begin with. What if we decide tonight that happiness has nothing to do with being good; it's about knowing exactly what we want. We can chose, Lindy, right now; you and me, and the rest of our life for second thoughts.

LINDY: (*Beat.*) He'll be here any minute.

ADAM: I don't care. I've been this good man; a good father, a good husband, a good provider, and good architect and I don't give a damn any more. Pack your bags.

LINDY: I'll come with you, I will. But not tonight. We have to do this right.

ADAM: You'll change your mind.

LINDY: Trust me, Adam. One week.

ADAM: Five days.

LINDY: (*Smiles.*) Five days.

ADAM: Four?

Their humour returns.

LINDY: You're insane.

ADAM: Look who's talking.

LINDY: (*Beat.*) This'll be headline news in Bicycle Monthly.

ADAM: Come here.

He starts forward to kiss her, but she slips away, needing to make some distance for the moment. She roots in her handbag and finds –

LINDY: (*An envelope.*) My poems.

ADAM: They were here all night.

LINDY: I wasn't sure I wanted you to know so much about me. (*Smiling.*) But now the cow's out of the bag.

ADAM: Is this 'instead of you'?

LINDY: And will you still want me five days from now? All that.

ADAM takes the poems.

LINDY dials.

ADAM: Don't bother calling a cab. I'll walk.

Someone at the other end picks up.

LINDY speaks with the authority of a country club matron.

LINDY: Desk? / Yes, someone left a food trolley in the hallway, would you please remove it. / I know normal room service hours, but it's disgraceful, a hotel of your standing to leave dangerous clutter in the hallway. / May I speak to the night manager? / I agree, there *is* no need for that. / Second floor. Thank you.

LINDY hangs up, turning to ADAM.

(*With a smirk.*) I'm a terror on committees.

She takes the trolley.

ADAM: (*Taking it.*) I'll do it. You should get dressed.

LINDY: (*Ignoring his offer to take the trolley out.*) A *man* wheeling a trolley from the room of Melinda Metz?! What would the neighbours say?

ADAM: Neighbours at five in the morning?

LINDY: Little by little one comes to realise that all the best people on earth are awake at this hour.

LINDY wheels the trolley to the door.

ADAM puts on his shoes.

She checks the hallway, then rolls out the trolley.

ADAM finds the cow and idly pushes its button a few times.

LINDY returns in her bare feet and supplies a sound effect.

'Mooo?'

She closes the door.

ADAM seems lost.

ADAM: Lindy –

LINDY: I have a whole other life to get straight in my head and only a few minutes to do it…

ADAM: You'll call?

She seems distracted.

LINDY: He'll be here any second, Adam, you must stay – go. I mean *go.* (*Trembling.*) I'm barely holding on here.

ADAM, with poems, peers out the door.

ADAM: All clear.

He opens the door wider.

LINDY leans towards him.

They kiss lightly. Then more. He breaks free.

(*Urgently.*) Come with me!

LINDY: Soon. I promise. For God sakes, Adam, go.

They stand in the open door, staring at each other, held in a motionless thrall.

The lights fade.

The End.